D1576484

WITHDRAWN

1 Sch.

1 Sch.

Claudia Schiffer
by
KARL LAGERFELD

Heinemann : London

About him,

I love his extraordinary talent, the hand that knows how to shape the most complex details but at the same time, exhibiting the most perfect simplicity.

I love the boldness of his designs, the enthusiasm he shares with all visions that he inhabits.

I love his extravagant irony, the funny stories he tells of his life that will put a smile on anyone's face.

About him,

I love his passion, that true fountain of youth which allows him to seduce and convince young and old alike, a renaissance artist who has somehow strayed into the twentieth century.

I love his elegance, his generosity, the complete assurance with which, every day, he shapes our taste.

I love Karl Lagerfeld.

Claudia Schiffer

1992

Berlin

1992

1993

1992

Amalfi

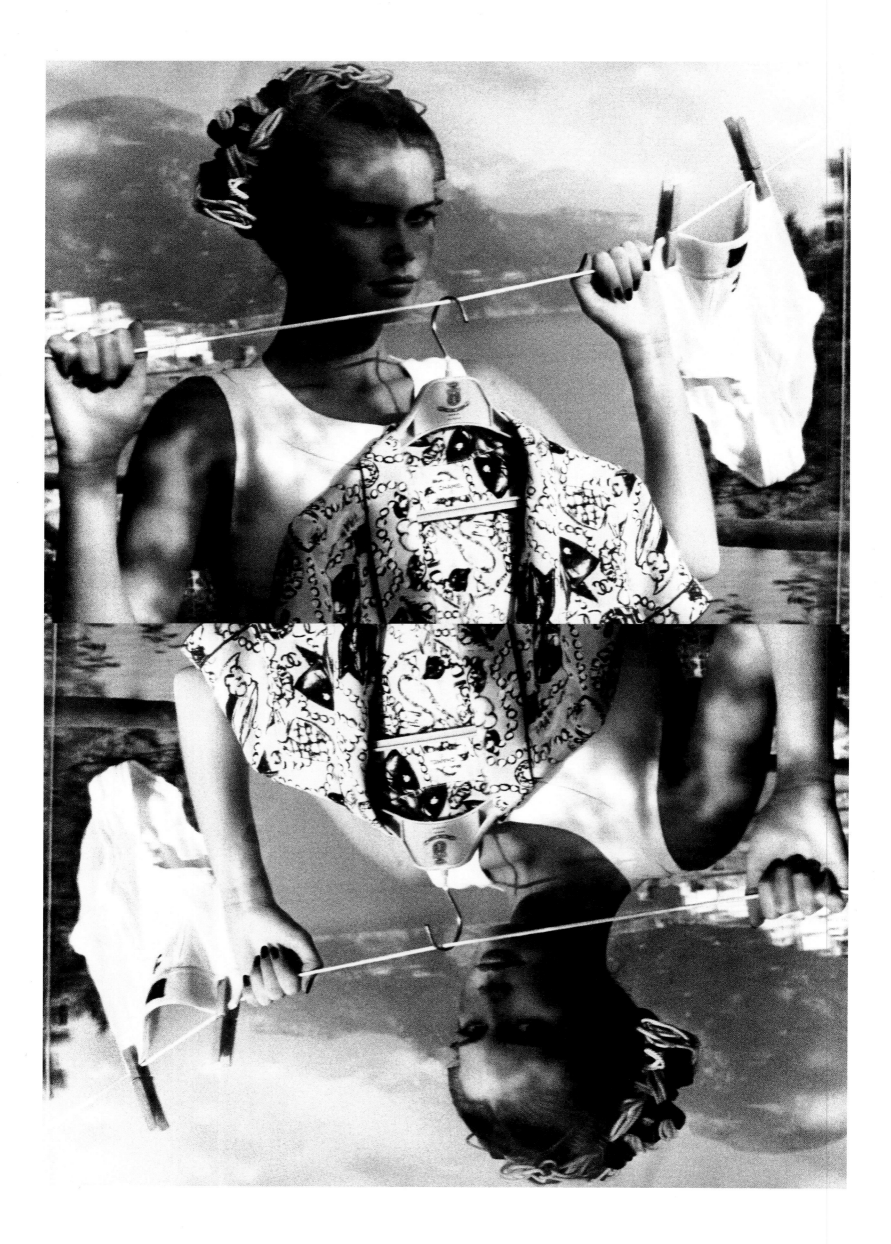

1992

1992

1991

Monte Carlo

1994

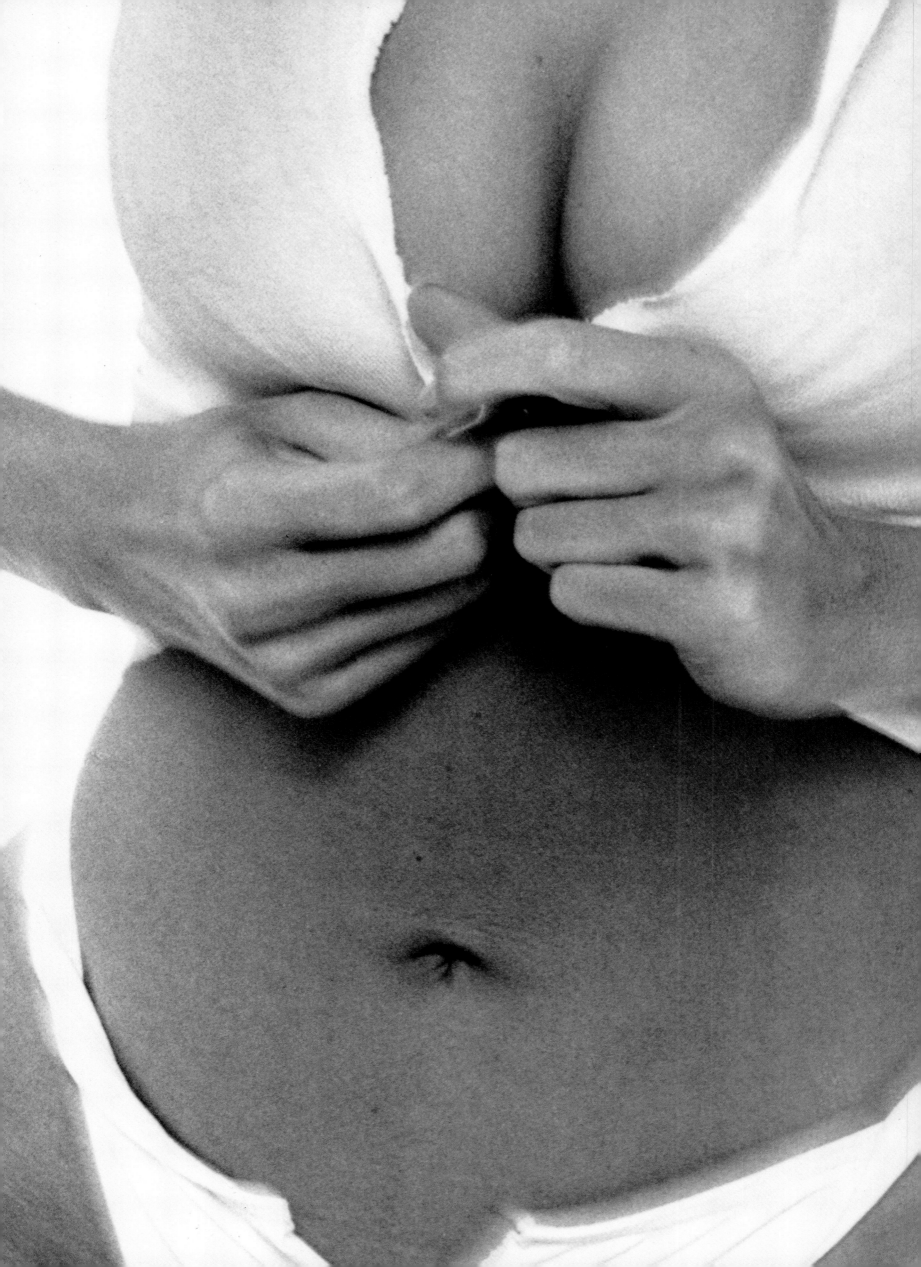

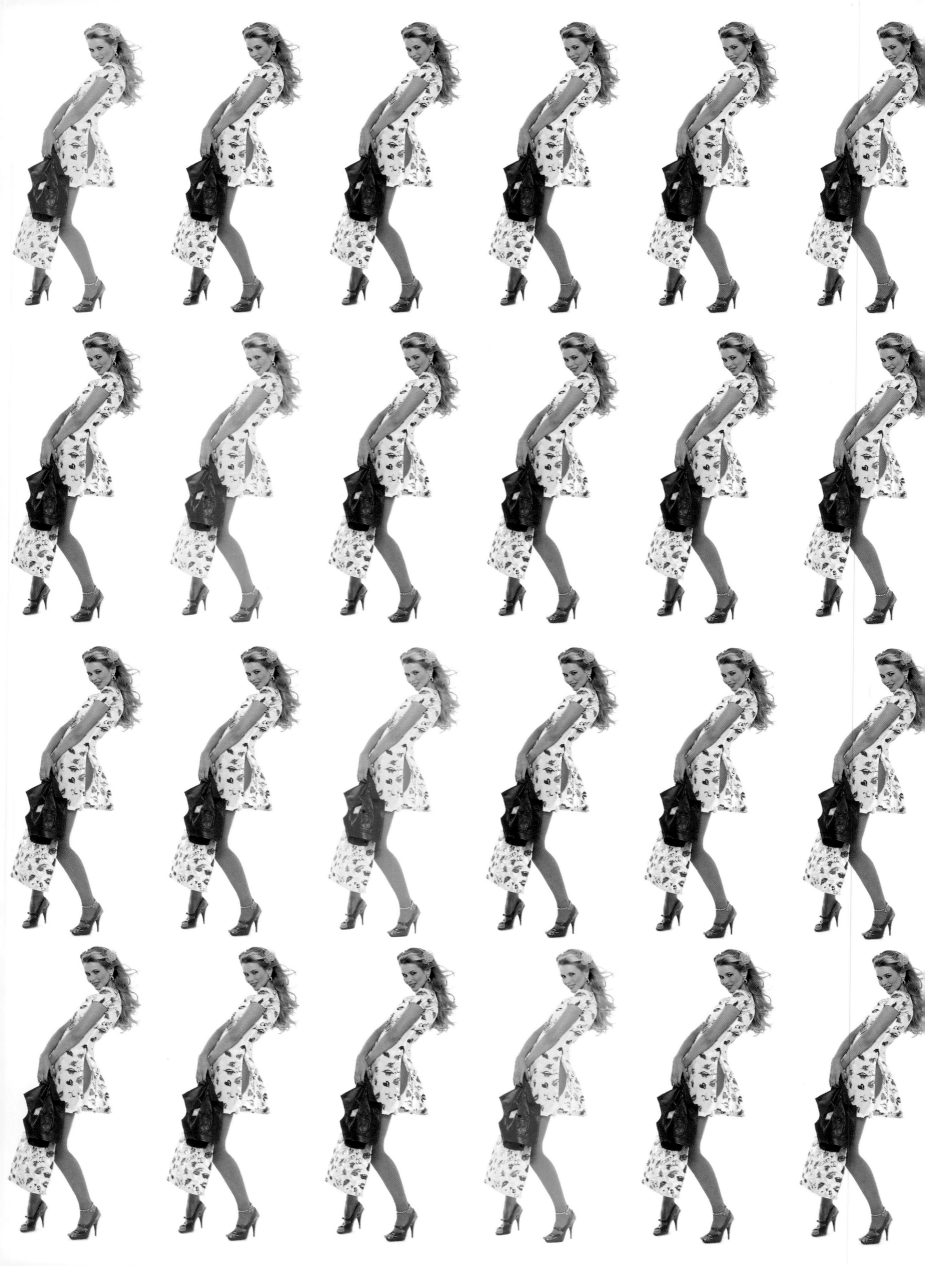

First published in Great Britain 1995 by William Heinemann Ltd, an imprint of Reed Consumer Books Ltd
Michelin House, 81 Fulham Road, London SW3 6RB and Auckland, Melbourne, Singapore and Toronto

© Édition°1, Hachette Group Livre, Paris 1995

A CIP catalogue record for this title is available from the British Library

ISBN 0 434 00261 5